AN INTRODUCTION TO

GOSPEL-CENTERED DISCIPLESHIP

An Introduction to Gospel-Centered Discipleship

Devoted: Discipleship Training for Small Groups

Copyright © 2018 by Clear Creek Community Church and Bruce Wesley, Yancey Arrington, and Ryan Lehtinen

Published by Clear Creek Resources

      A Ministry of Clear Creek Community Church

      999 North FM 270

      League City, Texas 77573

ISBN: 978-0-9979469-1-8

All rights reserved. No part of this publication may be reproduced, stored in a retrieval system or transmitted in any form by any means, electronic, mechanical, photocopy, recording or otherwise, without the prior permission of the publisher, except as provided by USA copyright law.

Unless otherwise indicated, all Scripture quotations are taken from:

The Holy Bible: English Standard Version, copyright © 2001 by Crossway Bibles, a division of Good News Publishers. Used by permission. All rights reserved.

All Scripture emphases have been added by the authors.

Printed in the United States of America

To the people of Clear Creek Community Church
who live to make disciples that make disciples.

CONTENTS

Acknowledgments

Introduction   11

Week 1: The Life of Following Jesus   13

Week 2: The Gospel Order of Growth   27

Week 3: A New Allegiance   41

Week 4: A New Responsibility   57

Week 5: A New Purpose   73

Week 6: Growth, Group, and Gospel Fluency   91

ACKNOWLEDGMENTS

The authors want to express their appreciation to Mandy Turner for her service as the editor on this project, and to Jon Coffey for additional editorial services.

Thanks goes to Brianna Coffey for design and artwork.

We also would like to extend our gratitude to the small groups who beta-tested this introduction and the feedback from the leaders of those groups.

AN INTRODUCTION TO **GOSPEL-CENTERED DISCIPLESHIP**

INTRODUCTION

Go therefore and make disciples of all nations, baptizing them in the name of the Father and of the Son and of the Holy Spirit, teaching them to observe all that I have commanded you

Matthew 28:19-20

Since its founding, Clear Creek Community Church has had one mission: to lead unchurched people to become fully devoted followers of Jesus Christ. This mission is simply a modern restating of Jesus' words in Matthew 28:19-20 where he commissioned his followers to "make disciples of all nations." In essence, Christ shows us what a Christian is to be — a disciple who makes disciples.

How are we to accomplish this mission? Should we just grab a Bible, cross our fingers, and hope to figure it out?

Fortunately, no. However, the reality is people cannot help lead others become fully devoted followers of Jesus if they haven't been trained to do so themselves.

Our purpose is to train you to be a disciple-making disciple!

This book is an introduction to the study series *Devoted: Discipleship Training for Small Groups* which outlines the training required in being the

INTRODUCTION

kind of disciple who gladly follows Christ's commission to "make disciples of all nations."

In this study you will be introduced to the *Spiritual Growth Grid* and how it plays a central role in CCCC's discipleship process. You will be introduced to three gospel storylines which provide the foundation for the essential beliefs and behaviors of a fully devoted follower of Jesus. You will also learn key concepts about gospel-centered growth and how they are applied to the Grid. This study contains further instruction on how members can make the most of their group experience by growing in their ability to apply the gospel to all of life. Finally, this book concludes with an orientation to what materials, timeline, and expectations come with studying the Devoted study series as a small group.

May the Lord use this in his grace to make us disciple-making disciples.

Grace to you,
The Elders of Clear Creek Community Church

01

THE LIFE OF FOLLOWING JESUS

Read each passage and record what each passage tells us about the Kingdom of God.

Mark 1:14-15

_____
_____
_____

Matthew 6:10

_____
_____
_____

Luke 17:20-21

_____
_____
_____

John 3:3-5

_____
_____
_____

Romans 14:17

_____
_____
_____

Follow me, and I will make

you become fishers of men.

—*Mark 1:17*

WEEK 1: THE LIFE OF FOLLOWING JESUS

01

Bill Gates made billions of dollars as the CEO of Microsoft. But in 2008, he redirected his focus away from the corporate world and toward philanthropy. Originally, he wanted to span the digital divide, but on a trip to Africa, he realized computers were not the greatest need of the children there, who lacked sufficient nutrition, health care, electricity, and adequate shelter. Since then, Bill and Melinda Gates have developed an impressive foundation with an endowment of over $44 billion that, for the last fifteen years, has focused on enhancing healthcare, reducing extreme poverty, and expanding educational opportunities and access to information technology. They have personally given more than $28 billion to the foundation.

Bill and Melinda Gates changed the object of their devotion from Microsoft to global transformation as evidenced by the way they use their time, energy, and $28 billion.

Devotion is common to all people, even if the object of their devotion varies. A religious person is devoted to the practices of his religion. A person devoted to the American Dream uses their time, talent, and money to build a sort of personal kingdom for their own happiness.

In this way, everyone is devoted to something, and the object of devotion is something that drives each person in the world to do what they do. It dictates the decisions they make, and guides the narrative of their lives.

AN INTRODUCTION TO **GOSPEL-CENTERED DISCIPLESHIP**

Everyone Lives Out a Storyline

The storyline of our lives is based on your beliefs. If we believe money is the path to happiness, that belief drives our storyline. If we believe success defines us, the storyline changes to match the belief. But through the gospel, God introduces to us a new storyline that is so significant that it calls each of us to reconsider our strategy for living.

> Now after John was arrested, Jesus came into Galilee, proclaiming the gospel of God, and saying, "The time is fulfilled, and the kingdom of God is at hand; repent and believe in the gospel."
>
> Mark 1:14-15

In a one-sentence sermon, Jesus announced a new opportunity followed by an appropriate response. What's the opportunity? The kingdom of God is at hand. And there is an appropriate way to respond to this opportunity — to repent and believe in the gospel.

The kingdom of God is at hand. This is the pivotal announcement of human history because it is where the storyline of our life joins in with God's storyline for all of creation. The kingdom is where people recognize the one true king and submit their life to him. God's kingdom is where God reigns. It's where humans are called to live the life God intended when he created us.

When you embrace the kingdom, you are embracing the fact that God wants to be part of every area of your life. You can't keep parts of your life out of the kingdom — separating your work life or sex life or family life from your spiritual life. As Abraham Kuyper famously stated, "There is not a square inch in the whole domain of our human existence over which Christ, who is Sovereign over all, does not cry, 'Mine!'"

WEEK 1: THE LIFE OF FOLLOWING JESUS

The Inside-Out Kingdom

To be clear, the reign of God is not the external political rule of a messianic leader. It is not getting the right person elected, or the right laws passed, or making sure that we are a Christian nation. Yes, we should be responsible citizens, but that's not how the kingdom of God comes.

Nor is God's kingdom about becoming more and more religious and controlling and creating rules for ourselves and those around us. Romans 14:17 says "For the kingdom of God is not a matter of eating and drinking, but of righteousness, peace and joy in the Holy Spirit." The essence of the kingdom of God is not a list of things you don't do. Sure, it might be wise for some to refrain from eating meat, drinking alcohol, wearing makeup, or gambling, but those choices don't qualify you for participation in the kingdom of God.

The kingdom of God is about the king himself coming to dwell in us by the power of the Holy Spirit. That's what happens when God, in the power of the Holy Spirit, takes up residence in a person. I (Bruce) remember when I first began to take following Jesus seriously. As I tried hard to do the things that I saw other Christians do, I focused on the outside, on my appearance, reputation and behaviors. But it was not until I began to rely on the power of God that was resident in me, that I found the strength to live as a follower of Jesus. I learned to depend on the power of Holy Spirit dwelling in me.

Jesus said, in Luke 17:21, "The kingdom of God is in the midst of you." The kingdom of God is an "inside-out" kingdom, not an "outside-in" kingdom. This was one of the hardest lessons for Jesus' disciples to learn. The kingdom is focused on the inner transformation of people who then transform the world. The good news is not that there is a kingdom, but rather, the proximity of the kingdom to us. Jesus came to make it possible for the reign of God to be available to people who thought the kingdom of God was a million miles away from them, or that they were disqualified by their sin. The kingdom of God is available as a gift of grace to carpenters, tax collectors, drug dealers, lawyers, prostitutes, engineers, scientists, salesmen and laborers along with everyone else. It is now possible for human beings to live in the presence of Jesus Christ free of guilt, filled with the power to face life with a sense of purpose, and to be at peace with themselves, others, and God.

This is the storyline that changes everything.

Experience the Kingdom of God

The way to kingdom living comes only when we repent of our sins and former storylines and believe in the gospel. Repentance and belief go together; you can't do one without the other. This is the response Jesus calls us to. We repent because it s now possible for people like us to live our lives under the reign and direction of God.

Repentance comes from two Greek words: meta noia. Literally, meta noia means to change your mind. Dallas Willard defined repentance as "reconsidering your strategy for living." He explained repentance this way:

> As a child I lived in southern Missouri where electricity was available only in the form of lightning. I remember the day that the power lines came near our farm and electricity became available to us. When the power lines came near our farm, a very different way of living presented itself. Our relationships to fundamental aspects of life — daylight and dark, hot and

cold, clean and dirty, work and leisure, preparing food and preserving it — could then be vastly changed for the better.
But we still had to believe in the electricity and its arrangements, understand them, and take the practical steps in relying on it. We had to repent, for electricity is at hand. We had to turn from kerosene lamps and iceboxes and cellars and woman powered sewing machines and radios with dry cell batteries. The power that could make life better was available — we simply had to rearrange our lives around electricity. We had to believe in it. This changed most everything.[1]

Repentance isn't merely admitting a fault, but completely reconsidering your strategy for living and rearranging your life to that end. It's what the Gates did when they stopped focusing on Microsoft and started working with their foundation.

By way of another example, there are a number of couples in our church who were living together before they got married. It was part of their strategy for developing a relationship. Some believed that marriage is such a great commitment that people should experiment with living as a married couple before getting married. They moved-in together, paid bills together, and slept together. They acted married in every way. But then they heard that Jesus had a different plan for them to prepare for marriage, and they reconsidered their strategy about dating, marriage, and sexuality. They moved apart and changed their sleeping arrangements because the kingdom of God — the will of God — is at hand. Others have reconsidered their strategies regarding business dealings or forgiveness of someone who hurt them, or have rearranged their financial commitments so they can prioritize giving to God and his purposes before they use their money for anything else.

---

[1] Willard, Dallas. *The Divine Conspiracy: Rediscovering Our Hidden Life in God.* San Francisco: HarperSanFrancisco, 1998, 30-31.

Belief and Devotion

Why would people change their whole lives for God? People repent because they believe the gospel is true. To be clear, our belief in the gospel is not that we are devoted to God, and as a result, he loves and forgives us, but rather, that God is devoted to us even when we were not devoted to him. God is devoted to us first. He loved us first.

Here's how:
- God is devoted to us by sending his Son to take our sin on the cross, providing a way for us to be forgiven and reconciled to God.

- God is devoted to us by giving us the Holy Spirit to dwell in us, convict us, guide us into truth, and give us power for living.

- God is devoted to us by putting us in a community where we are loved, served, and celebrated.

- God is devoted to us by giving us his Word, the Bible, in which he reveals himself and his will.

When we become aware of how much God loves us in Christ, and that he has made his kingdom available to us, we repent and believe in the gospel. This is how God changes the storyline of our lives.

The Spiritual Growth Grid

Many believers are unable to point to anyone who has intentionally committed to helping them grow as a disciple. But that's precisely what

WEEK 1: THE LIFE OF FOLLOWING JESUS

Jesus did. Jesus led a small group of twelve — he was a leader who trained his followers to rearrange their lives to follow him.

Jesus did not lead his disciples to change the world like Bill Gates. He called them to serve people, but that wasn't the ultimate focus.

Jesus didn't lead them to be religious with a list of do's and don'ts. He insisted that they not focus on transforming their lives from the outside in.

Jesus did not lead his disciples to just try to live comfortably, fulfilling their own dreams in pursuit of the American Dream.

He refused to let them settle for any of these things. He provided a greater storyline. People were created with the purpose of knowing God and walking with him, living a life submitted to God as part of his kingdom.

If we distill all that Jesus taught, three categories emerge:

Listen & Obey: God is speaking, guiding, and directing; we must rearrange our lives so we will listen and obey.

Love & Serve: God gave us spiritual gifts and a familial connection with other Christians; we must rearrange our lives to engage with God's people.

Go & Multiply: God is at work throughout the world; we rearrange our lives because God sends his disciples into the world to make disciples.

AN INTRODUCTION TO **GOSPEL-CENTERED DISCIPLESHIP**

Martin Luther learned that self-inflicted wounds of penitence did not give him peace or a favorable standing with God. He learned and believed that his comfort and hope lay in the truth that Christ Jesus was wounded for his transgressions. Roughly 500 years ago, Luther initiated the Protestant Reformation when he nailed a piece of paper to a door that held 95 statements about the Christian faith which he wanted to debate with his colleagues. The first stated, "When our Lord and Master Jesus Christ said 'Repent,' he intended that the entire life of believers should be repentance." Luther was not saying that we should live our whole lives feeling guilty about something, but rather, when we embrace a pervasive all-of-life-is-repentance perspective, it's the best sign that we are growing deeply in the character of Jesus. Just as we began our journey of faith with turning from our former ways and trusting in Jesus for salvation, so we must daily repent and believe. This is the life of a disciple of Jesus.

01

WEEKLY EXERCISE

Make a list of the things or people to whom you are devoted. For each thing you listed, write out ways you have rearranged your life to include that thing or person (i.e. what does your devotion look like?).

I AM DEVOTED TO...	HOW I REARRANGE MY LIFE
_____	_____
_____	_____
_____	_____
_____	_____
_____	_____

Write out two specific things you will do to grow in your devotion to Jesus this week.

1.
_____
_____

2.
_____
_____

02

THE GOSPEL ORDER OF GROWTH

Read Genesis 1:27, 2:15-17

What does this tell us about mankind's creation?
_____
_____
_____

How do God's statements define the identity of Adam and Eve?
_____
_____
_____

What was so good about God's pronouncement concerning Adam and Eve?
_____
_____
_____

What was their God-ordained role given to them in Gen. 2:15-17?
_____
_____
_____

What does God's warning to Adam and Eve say about their identity as well?
_____
_____
_____

I have been crucified with Christ. It is no longer I who live, but Christ who lives in me. And the life I now live in the flesh I live by faith in the Son of God, who loved me and gave himself for me.

—Galatians 2:20

WEEK 2: THE GOSPEL ORDER OF GROWTH

02

If repentance and belief is the way we enter into the life of following Jesus, what happens after we become followers of Jesus? When we examine the everyday logistics of living a devoted life, we need to be aware the gospel has a specific order which impacts spiritual growth:

Identity Informs Activity
(who we are determines what we do)

However, as products of the culture in which we live, we've been trained to think differently. There's a scene in Christopher Nolan's movie *Batman Begins* where Katie Holmes' character asks Batman what his name is, to which he replies, "It's not who I am underneath, but what I do that defines me." Many who watch movie will nod their heads in agreement thinking, *Batman said that, so it must be right!* According to the Caped Crusader, what we do determines who we are. In other words, he says activity informs identity.

If someone came up to you and said, "Who are you?" most would respond with their occupation. Because of this subconscious cultural mindset, most people don't think who we are determines what we do but the other way around. This type of thinking even trickles down into how people think about spiritual growth.

AN INTRODUCTION TO **GOSPEL-CENTERED DISCIPLESHIP**

The Right and Wrong Way to Grow Spiritually

This was true in my spiritual upbringing. I (Yancey) became a follower of Jesus at ten years of age. When I did, I was then given a little booklet and told, "Now you need to do all the stuff in here." So I began to think that being a Christian was really about becoming a person who reads the Bible, prays, and does other things. I began to see my identity as a Christian based on my behavior. As you might imagine, when I was doing well concerning obedience I felt good about myself. But when I struggled with sin or was lax on my spiritual disciplines, I felt like less of a Christian. I was living as if my activity informed my identity.

In the previous lesson you were introduced to three different pairs of behaviors that describe a follower of Jesus — listen and obey, love and serve, and go and multiply. Now, some might say, "Just do these behaviors, and you've got it. So, go and do them!" The focus is solely on behavior, and those concepts can move from being statements meant to encourage our growth, to statements that crush us with guilt.

This is because our performance becomes the foundation for our identity. If we're good at this, we can check the boxes, we can do the deeds, and we may even begin to believe that somehow we're better than others because of it. But it can also make us despair. We can get frustrated and depressed because we're not good at it. We stumble and fall. We blow it. And somehow we believe that we are worse than others in God's eyes because we don't perform well. All of this is a result of believing that what we do determines who we are. And that reversal is not only unbiblical, it's satanic and as old as the Garden of Eden.

WEEK 2: THE GOSPEL ORDER OF GROWTH

A Lesson From The Garden

Genesis 1:27 says, "So God created man in his own image, in the image of God he created him; male and female he created them." God says Adam and Eve are made in his image. That is their god-given reality. After God tells them who they are, then God gives them a command:

> *The Lord God took the man and put him in the garden of Eden to work it and keep it. And the Lord God commanded the man, saying, "You may surely eat of every tree of the garden, but of the tree of the knowledge of good and evil you shall not eat, for in the day that you eat of it you shall surely die.*
>
> Genesis 2:15-17

Do you see the order? Their identity as God's image-bearers informs their activity of stewarding the earth. Adam and Eve have been given one thing they're not supposed to do. They have everything they need. Then the serpent, Satan, tempts Adam and Eve to eat of the forbidden tree.

> *He said to the woman, "Did God actually say, 'You shall not eat of any tree in the garden'?" And the woman said to the serpent, "We may eat of the fruit of the trees in the garden, but God said, 'You shall not eat of the fruit of the tree that is in the midst of the garden, neither shall you touch it, lest you die.'" But the serpent said to the woman, "You will not surely die. For God knows that when you eat of it [activity] your eyes will be opened, and you will be like God [identity], knowing good and evil."*
>
> Genesis 3:1b-5

Satan challenged Adam and Eve to doubt what God had said about them.

They were tempted to believe they were something less than they needed to be, and that the key to achieving their identity would only be found in an action: eating the fruit that had been forbidden. The order is reversed. It's the beginning of the anti-gospel message.

As pastor and author Jeff Vandersteldt notes, Satan's message to Adam and Eve in the Garden is "What you do will save you," and that makes up the very fabric of worldliness. Again, that's why we're so used to defining ourselves by our activity. *I'm a parent. I'm a daughter. I'm a teacher. I'm a student. I'm an engineer. I'm a pastor. I'm a Longhorn. I'm an Aggie.* Vandersteldt says, "The lie is we are nothing apart from what we do. The reality is we are who we are, not because of what we do, but because of what God has done."[1] This is not only the truth of the gospel but also why getting the correct order is important in developing our devotion as followers of Jesus.

The Rubric of Gospel Growth

A rubric is a heading or idea under which everything else falls; it's a way to interpret the rest of something. The Spiritual Growth Grid is a rubric of gospel growth. The main movements we must learn in order to understand gospel-centered growth are as follows:

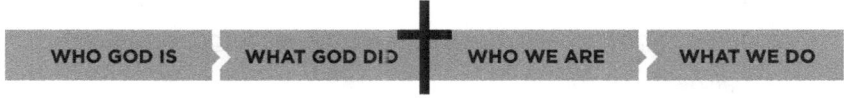

We begin with "Who God Is," which leads us to "What God Did" (specifically Jesus' saving work at the cross). That gospel work now determines

---

[1] "Soma School | What Is the Church? | Gospel Foundation." YouTube. 2014. Accessed October 03, 2016. https://youtu.be/GEfm57qHEbg.

WEEK 2: THE GOSPEL ORDER OF GROWTH

"Who We Are" and that new identity informs "What We Do." Do you see the gospel order here? Who God is and what he has done in Jesus gives us our identity which in turn leads to our activity.

This is the pattern repeated in the Bible. Almost every command in the New Testament is given in light of who we are in Jesus. For example, take these words Paul wrote to the Colossians:

> *If then you have been raised with Christ, seek the things that are above, where Christ is, seated at the right hand of God. Set your minds on things that are above, not on things that are on earth. For you have died, and your life is hidden with Christ in God.*
>
> Colossians 3:1-3

Our identity as believers — those who have been raised with Christ and whose lives are hidden with Christ in God — is the determining factor at the root of our activity. It is why we seek to set our minds on the things that are above.

Paul continues in verses 12-13:

> *Put on then, as God's chosen ones, holy and beloved, compassionate hearts, kindness, humility, meekness, and patience, bearing with one another and, if one has a complaint against another, forgiving each other; as the Lord has forgiven you, so you also must forgive.*

Again, we see activity rooted in our identity. Since you are "God's chosen ones, holy and beloved", you will then "put on" these behaviors: "compassionate hearts, kindness, humility, meekness, and patience." This order is so important because our identity is no longer grounded upon our behavior. It's founded upon something greater: what God has already done for us in Jesus, or what we know as the gospel.

So all these activities of a follower of Jesus as listed on the Spiritual Growth Grid (Listen & Obey, Love & Serve, Go & Multiply) don't hang over our head to build our pride or deepen our despair. Instead, they are natural — or really, supernatural — extensions of who we are in Jesus. If not, then being devoted will only be fueled by our willpower and tenacity. But since these behaviors are established by our gospel identity, there is only one way we can truly embrace devotion well: faith.

The Continuing Practice of Repenting & Believing

Romans 1:16 says, "For I am not ashamed of the gospel, for it is the power of God for salvation to everyone who *believes*, to the Jew first and also to the Greek." Do you want to experience the power of God in your salvation? As Paul says here, this comes to us by belief. It's not just a one-time belief when we begin a relationship with Jesus, but a daily exercising of faith. This means that our entire understanding of what the gospel gives to us — our identity and our activity – is completely based on faith. We take it by faith that Jesus has given us this identity.

Therefore, works don't establish our identity. On the contrary, we take hold of our identity by faith.

In Galatians 2:20, Paul says, "I have been crucified with Christ. It is no longer I who live, but Christ who lives in me. And the life I now live in the flesh I live by faith in the Son of God, who loved me and gave himself for me." Paul says we live by faith in who Jesus is, and what he has done for us in the gospel.

Most of our problems in growing our devotion to Jesus aren't due to not knowing, but not believing what we already know. That's why a huge step in being devoted is repenting from our mindset that what we do makes us who we are and believing that God has given us, in Christ, our identity which leads us to certain activities. That's the gospel order of growth – the order that must be taken by faith.

My (Yancey) father was an outspoken atheist until he became a follower of Jesus at 42 years old. Up to that point he partied hard and lived hard. Years ago I remember visiting my parents and looking through one of the many different photo albums my mom has assembled over the years. As I was looking through one from my childhood, I noticed my father was looking at them with me. Those images of us fishing together, playing basketball, and other slices of life brought smiles to both of our faces. And then I turned the page and found a photo of my father at a party. With a beer in one hand and a cigarette in the other, his face proclaimed that he was on the bad end of the festivities. Eyes glassed over, a crooked mouth, and slumped posture gave him away. He was bombed. I turned to look at my dad and saw his eyes narrow and the smile turn into the pressed lips of determination. Then my dad pointed to himself in the photo and said, "Son, I don't know him anymore. That man is dead."

My father's favorite verse has become one of mine as well. It expresses the truth of the gospel for those who want to be devoted to God. 2 Corinthians 5:17 says, "Therefore, if anyone is in Christ, he is a new creation. The old has passed away; behold, the new has come."

The gospel order matters: Identity Informs Activity (who we are determines what we do).

In Christ, you become a new person with a new identity which leads to a new activity. This change of identity does not come from what you do, but by faith in what Christ has done through his work at the cross.

02

WEEKLY EXERCISE

Getting the identity-activity order right has to do with our motivation. Why do we do what we do? Explain how your identity as a follower of Jesus ought to motivate or inform each of the following five activities.

Activity: Reading the Bible

How does my identity motivate me?

_____
_____
_____

Activity: Praying

How does my identity motivate me?

_____
_____
_____

Activity: Attending Worship Services

How does my identity motivate me?

_____
_____
_____

Activity: Being in a Small Group

How does my identity motivate me?

_____
_____
_____

Activity: Sharing the Gospel

How does my identity motivate me?

_____
_____
_____

03

A NEW ALLEGIANCE

Read Hebrews 11:8-10

How do you think God spoke to Abraham to "call" him?

_____
_____
_____

What are some of the ways that God speaks to people today?

_____
_____
_____

What were the challenges to obeying God for Abraham?

_____
_____
_____

What does this passage teach us about living a life where we listen and obey?

_____
_____
_____

So then you are no longer strangers and aliens, but you are fellow citizens with the saints and members of the household of God.

—*Ephesians 2:19*

WEEK 3: A NEW ALLEGIANCE

03

There is always a story behind what you do. You know this if you are a parent. Your seven-year-old comes crying to you that his brother pushed him down. You go to his brother and he has a story. Maybe it's, "He destroyed my LEGO creation," or "A pterodactyl was going to eat him, so I pushed him down to save him." There is always a story.

The same is true for adults. There is always a reason behind our actions. And if you want to know the reason, you have to know the story. The story explains what you believe about God and what you believe about your own identity. And if you want to change the way you act, you have to reconsider what you believe about who God is, what he has done in Jesus, and who you are as a result. Identity informs activity.

So, when it comes to Christianity, there is a storyline behind the behavior of Christ-followers as they listen and obey; a story of good news based on who God is and what God did for us, in Christ, which gives us a new identity. The first gospel storyline starts with recognizing God as King

God Is King

God reveals who he is in the Bible. From beginning to end, it's clear that God is the ultimate leader, the sovereign of the universe who has final authority. In the world of the Bible, a person of this nature was a king. Look at some of the ways God is described in the book of Psalms:

> *For God is the King of all the earth; sing praises with a psalm!*
>
> Psalm 47:7

> *For the Lord is a great God, and a great King above all gods.*
>
> Psalm 95:3

> *I will extol you, my God and King, and bless your name forever and ever... Your kingdom is an everlasting kingdom, and your dominion endures throughout all generations.*
>
> Psalm 145:1, 13

Why should God be king? It's not just because he is the creator, the one who orders the universe and has power to do as he wills, it's also because God is good. God is so devoted to us being in his kingdom that the Bible is filled with stories about the work of God to rescue people who have rejected him, disobeyed him, and defiled his name. He is the kind of king who transforms his enemies into citizens of his kingdom which is characterized by righteousness, peace, and joy.

God loves us. He knows us better than we know ourselves. He has all wisdom to lead us to live life to the fullest — for our good and for his glory. Armed with this perfect love and infinite wisdom, he calls us to what is right and best for us.

A Called People

As king, God called a people to be his people. He called Abraham to leave his country for a country God would later show him. He called Moses through a burning bush. He called the children of Israel, and twelve disciples to follow him.

God called, and he is calling still. If you are a follower of Jesus you have heard this call; probably not through a burning bush, but from someone sharing the gospel with you.

But what is he calling us to?

> He has delivered us from the domain of darkness and transferred us to the kingdom of his beloved Son, in whom we have redemption, the forgiveness of sins. (Colossians 1:13-14)

This shows what God did for us in Christ on the cross. He delivered us from the domain of darkness in which we were slaves to sin, and transferred us to the kingdom of his beloved Son, Jesus. Everyone in God's kingdom has been rescued and delivered. He gives us a new identity as citizens — forgiven and set free.

Called to be Citizens

It's a big deal to be a citizen. A young man in our church came from a war-torn country where he escaped life as a child soldier. He was separated from his family and lived in a refugee camp until he was brought to the United States. He was in the country legally but was not a citizen because this was not his country. After years in the U.S., a friend helped him work through the citizenship process. At the ceremony where he became a citizen, he did what every American kid did every day at school, growing up: he pledged allegiance to the flag.

> I pledge allegiance to the flag of the United States of America, and to the republic for which it stands, one nation under God, indivisible, with liberty and justice for all.

By saying these words, he was declaring his new identity as a United States citizen for whom there is unity, freedom, and justice.

How do we, as Americans, demonstrate our allegiance? We listen to our authorities and obey them. We demonstrate obedience in the way we drive, pay taxes, defend our nation, and myriads of other instances. Some people are good citizens and some are bad citizens. But even the bad ones are still citizens; it's their identity.

When we receive Christ's work on the cross for us, God takes his rightful place as the one true king of our lives, and gives us a new identity.

God gives us citizenship immediately through our faith in Jesus no matter what we have done, good or bad. We don't earn citizenship. We can't buy citizenship in God's kingdom. It's a gift of grace. As citizens in God's kingdom, we have the presence and power of God in our lives in the person of the Holy Spirit through whom God has made it possible for us to know his will, hear his voice, and obey him.

God is our good King who called us into his kingdom by delivering us from the domain of darkness and transferring us into his kingdom. As citizens, we listen and obey.

Listen & Obey

I (Bruce) heard a pastor tell the story about being in second grade when his teacher read a story from the Old Testament about a man named Eli —

an older worker in the Temple — and a young boy named Samuel, whom Eli mentored. As the story goes in Samuel, one night after Samuel had gone to bed, he thought he heard Eli calling for him. He got out of bed, ran to where Eli was lying down and said, "I heard you call. Here I am."

"I didn't call you," Eli said. "Go back to bed." Samuel complied. But moments later, he heard his name again. "Samuel!" the voice called. Samuel rose from his bed, hurried to Eli's side and said, "Here I am; you called me." Again Eli told the boy he was wrong. Again Samuel returned to his bed. When it happened a third time, the old man finally realized what was going on.

"Samuel, maybe God is trying to get a message to you," Eli explained. "Go back and lie down. If the voice calls again, say, 'Speak, God. I am your servant, ready to listen.'"

And so, the text says, "Samuel returned to his bed," where soon thereafter he heard his name yet again. "Samuel! Samuel!" the Lord called, to which Samuel replied on cue, "Speak, for your servant is listening."

God, indeed, spoke to young Samuel an important message for his people. As a boy, the pastor was amazed that God spoke to a little boy. So when it came time for recess, instead of running onto the playground, he asked his teacher, "Does God still speak to little boys?" She smiled. Placing her two hands on his small shoulders, she looked him square in the eye.

"Oh, yes," she said. "He most certainly does. And if you learn to quiet yourself and listen, he even will speak to you. I am sure of it." Then she reached in her desk and gave him a little poem to read and think about.

> Oh, give me Samuel's ear
> An open ear, O Lord,

> Alive and quick to hear
> Each whisper of Thy Word;
> Like him to answer to Your call,
> And to obey You first of all.

When I heard the story, I had three little girls at home and I was moved to tears by the thought that the God of heaven would speak to them. I imagined what it might be like for them to hear God's whisper in their hearts; for them to know God as a good King who called and made a way for them to be citizens in his eternal kingdom. And I began to tell them, "The most satisfying thing in all the world is to hear the voice of God. The most exciting thing is to obey his voice."

Throughout the Bible, God spoke through angels, dreams, burning bushes, people, and ultimately through his Son, Jesus, who is the living Word of God. By his providence, we have the written Word of God. And God is still speaking to us today.

God can speak to our hearts today. If you lower the ambient noise in your life and listen expectantly for his voice through his Word and the witness of his Spirit, you realize God still speaks. He speaks about our priorities, relationships, kids, sexuality, money, jobs, and purpose in the world. God speaks about the biggest problems in your life. And when he speaks, we obey. This is what citizens do. They demonstrate their allegiance to the king when they listen and obey!

Work Backwards Through the Story

What happens when we don't listen and obey? We can wallow in guilt. We might beat ourselves up. We can give in to doubt. But here is what disciples of Jesus do when they struggle to listen and obey: They work backwards through the story.

Working backwards through a gospel storyline begins by assessing our behavior (What We Do), then moves to beliefs connected to that behavior (Who God Is, What God Did, Who We Are), looking for areas where we may need to deepen our trust.

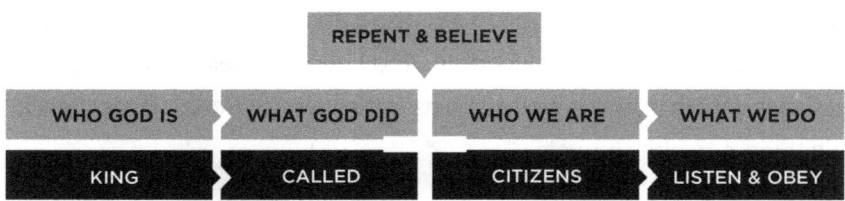

For example, if someone struggles with an area of obedience, we can help him or her by asking how clearly they see themselves as a citizen. Then we might ask how deeply they believe God has called them into his kingdom. Finally, we can press into their hearts to see if they currently view God as their King. With each step backwards into the gospel storyline we are trying to identify which gospel truths their heart struggles to believe. Again, it's always belief before behavior. True change must happen at the heart level and working backwards can help identify which truths we are, or aren't, believing deeply.

Finding out the answers leads us to repent and believe, and rearrange our lives to:

1. Experience Worship in Community
You might go fish on the lake or hike in the mountains and consider that worship. After all, you see the beauty of creation, the order of the universe, and those are good things to praise God for. But if we worship in community, we are reminded of the character of God in the songs we sing, the

scriptures we read, and the stories we tell. We are reminded that God is powerful, holy, faithful, loving, forgiving, generous, merciful, and eternal. This is what worship is all about. It's remembering and declaring the kind of King our God is. Together, we help each other worship well.

2. Surrender Our Will in Prayer
Jesus taught us to pray in Matthew 6:10, "Your kingdom come, your will be done, on earth as it is in heaven." He knew God's rule over our lives is what we need most, but we must acknowledge our desire for control. Samuel prayed, "Speak, Lord, your servant is listening." He was saying, "I am waiting for you to speak, and I will immediately obey your word." In prayer, we accept God's plans and surrender to his will for our lives.

3. Hear God's Voice
One of our sayings at CCCC is, "We open our Bible, and God opens his mouth." God speaks most often and most clearly through the Bible. When we sit down to read the Bible, we should always pray, "God, please speak to me." And God will speak in those quiet moments when we are silent enough to hear.

As you continue the journey with CCCC, you will learn to study, understand, and apply the words of God to the challenges of life. You can listen and obey God through the Bible.

Remember Your Place in the Story

God is a good king. In the gospel, he has called you, transferred you into his kingdom, and made you a citizen. Rearrange your life activities around the good news of your new gospel identity. As a citizen in God's kingdom, we repent and believe by placing ourselves under his good rule. In this way, we are deciding in advance that God's way is the best way and his words lead to life.

> *So then, you are no longer strangers and aliens, but you are fellow citizens with the saints and members of the household of God.*
>
> Ephesians 2:19

03

WEEKLY EXERCISE

Listening and obeying begins with hearing from God. One of the best ways to hear from God is by reading the Bible. Create a plan that will help you read the Bible more regularly.

Think about when, where, and how often you will read the Bible.

_____
_____
_____

With whom will you discuss what you are reading?

_____
_____
_____

Choose a Bible reading plan on the Bible app or at esv.org/biblereadingplans, and begin reading today.

_____
_____
_____

A NEW RESPONSIBILITY

Read Galatians 4:4-7

What does verse 5 say is the point of our redemption?

_____

_____

_____

What does it mean to "receive adoption as sons"?

_____

_____

_____

What, in verse 6, is the result of being God's children?

_____

_____

_____

What does the word "Abba" tell us about our relationship to God as Father?

_____

_____

_____

What is the contrast made in verse 7? What are the differences between the two?

_____

_____

_____

But when the fullness of time had come, God sent forth his Son, born of woman, born under the law, to redeem those who were under the law, so that we might receive adoption as sons. And because you are sons, God has sent the Spirit of his Son into our hearts, crying, 'Abba! Father!' So you are no longer a slave, but a son, and if a son, then an heir through God.

—Galatians 4:4-7

04

WEEK 4: A NEW RESPONSIBILITY

Living in the culture we do today, the temptation is to view each other in the local church just like we would regard the people in any other social group. Maybe you've gotten to know the families of the kids who play on your kid's sports team. It could be that you get together with some friends for a monthly game night, or even that you've become such a regular at your local coffee shop that you're considered part of the group.

There's nothing wrong with those groups. We should be part of them. But they all share a common characteristic. They all have a relatively low level of commitment to the other people within the group.

For example, if one of the dads is going crazy and acting like a fool at your kid's baseball game, you may not feel the need to correct him but will probably move to the other side of the stands. Or if someone at your poker night says something about going through a hard time in their marriage, you might commiserate but not feel any real need to help them. Or if one of the regulars at the coffee shop took your favorite seat and won't give it up, you don't have to work it out, you can sit somewhere else, come back another day, or just go to the next coffee shop across the street.

We wouldn't think twice about any of those decisions. The level of commitment is appropriate to the type of group. Unfortunately, that same level of commitment is common in the church.

AN INTRODUCTION TO **GOSPEL-CENTERED DISCIPLESHIP**

Many followers of Jesus, if they suddenly have a problem with someone at church, will simply sit in a different seat, attend a different service, or even move to a different campus rather than actually work through those issues. They treat church like their coffee shop. It's a place they go, not necessarily a community they're a part of. They relate to the people at church just like any other social group in their life. And this doesn't just happen in church services, but in church small groups as well.

What do you do with the person in your group who uses group time as their chance to vent and gripe about the people in their life? Maybe they're always complaining about others, and they're constantly crossing over the line from talking about a situation that truly needs prayer to just gossiping about somebody that they're upset with. How do you talk to them in a way that helps them grow?

This second gospel storyline can help us understand what a community of Christ-followers should look like by, once again, pointing us to our identity in Jesus. Let's walk through it.

God as Father

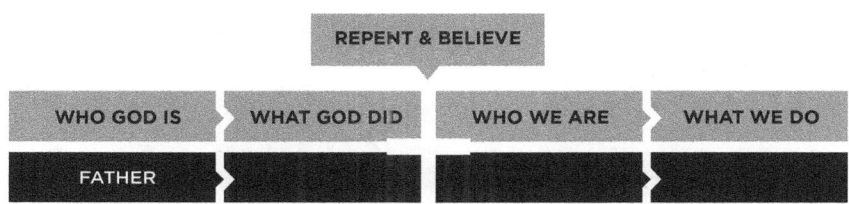

Genesis begins with a picture of God as the all-powerful Creator, as he creates the heavens and earth by his spoken word. In creating Adam and Eve, he initiates a relationship with them. From the very beginning we get a picture of God who, although the father metaphor is not explicitly described, is clearly relational.

The relationship he established was not only a vertical relationship between him and his people but a horizontal relationship between one another as well. He designed Adam and Eve to perfectly complement, deeply love, and faithfully care for each other, modeled after the way he cared for them.

But in Genesis 3, we see the Fall happen and sin enter the story. It's described as a fracturing of relationships. The vertical relationship between God and his people is broken. Adam and Eve are cast out of the garden. Likewise, the horizontal relationship between his people is broken. In the aftermath of the fall, God said that from then on there would be struggle and strife in humans' relationships with each other that they had never experienced before.

And throughout the rest of the Bible we see the story unfold of God initiating and pursuing the reconciliation of those fractured relationships, which ultimately culminates in the person of Jesus Christ.

When we get to Jesus, the Fatherhood of God and his relationship with his people takes on new meaning. There's a reason why Jesus' favorite way to address or refer to God was by calling him "Father." It's clear that in him there's a new way to relate to God.

Adopted Sons

Adoption means you become part of the family. You're no longer the outsider. You have a home and a father. When you are adopted, you are given all the powers, privileges, and protections of a natural born child.

Let's look at how Paul describes what happens when you become a follower of Jesus:

> But when the fullness of time had come, God sent forth his Son, born of woman, born under the law, to redeem those who were under the law, so that we might receive adoption as sons. And because you are sons, God has sent the Spirit of his Son into our hearts, crying, 'Abba! Father!' So you are no longer a slave, but a son, and if a son, then an heir through God.
>
> Galatians 4:4-7

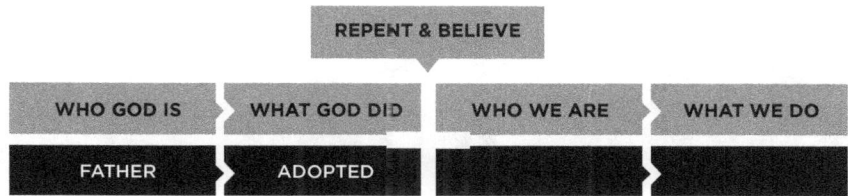

Notice how Paul doesn't say you become a "child", or even "sons and daughters." He says, "Son." In this context, there is something significant in being a son. In Paul's time, adoption meant the same thing as it does today but family hierarchies were different. Sons got the bulk of their father's inheritance. Daughters would be taken care of by their husbands, who had an inheritance coming to them. Sons were to carry on their father's legacy and riches. As a follower of Jesus, you are a son, God is your Father. This means you are the heir of his riches.

It's worth mentioning that some people did not have had a good father growing up. To call God a father is not a flattering description. It's like calling God a four-lettered word. But whether you had a good earthly father or not, God is an infinitely better father than the father you grew up with.

He loves you, provides for you, and protects you in a way no earthly father can. He is the perfect Father you never had. Paul says that our hearts cry out "Abba! Father!" which is what children would call their fathers. It's an intimate and personal title; something like calling God, "Dearest Father."

And you are not an only child. You are part of a family. That's your new identity. The Father has adopted you into His family.

A New Family, A New Responsibility

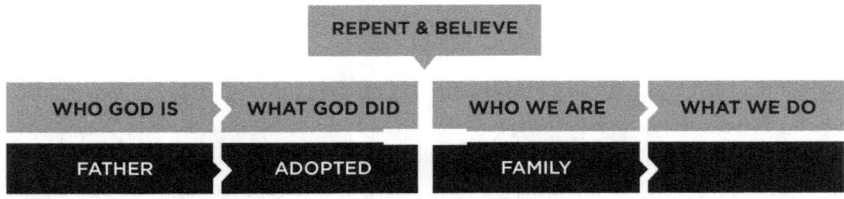

When God the Father adopts us into his family, that new relationship comes with wonderful privileges. You are an heir in God's kingdom. But not only that, we find ourselves now with a new responsibility to the other members of that family — the Church.

That's how we view all believers worldwide and how we view our local community of Christ-followers.

As a father of three kids, I (Ryan) have a responsibility to my family. My time isn't just my time. When I get home from work, I take a breath at the door, and my second shift starts. That means I'm going to play, help with dinner, give baths, or do whatever needs to get done. I have a responsibility to my family. And it's not just me, it's everyone in my family. My wife has responsibilities. Even my kids have responsibilities to family. That's part of being a family. Each person has a responsibility to everyone else.

This is what makes the local church different than our sports families, game night friends, or coffee shop regulars. We have a fundamentally different relationship to each other. The difference is rooted in our identity given to us by the gospel. Because of the work of Jesus on the cross, there is now a reconciliation of the two types of relationships that were fractured in Genesis. There's a restored vertical relationship between us and God and a new horizontal relationship between us and the rest of his people. Jesus gave his life for us to be family. And with family comes responsibility.

Love & Serve

So how do we live out the responsibility we have to our new family?

It's pretty simple: we love and serve one another.

Isn't that what a healthy family looks like? They care for one another. They don't speak ill, but well, of one another. They use their gifts to serve each other. They carry the financial load of the family. They handle conflict in godly ways with an aim for mutual growth. Families love and serve each other, even when loving and serving each other isn't easy.

That's why small groups are so important. They are places where we can love and be loved, serve and be served. It's also why we have hundreds of people serving in ministry; not because the staff is lazy, but because it gets more of the family involved. It's why we have adults who don't have little kids but are serving little kids. They see this as a family responsibility. It's why many people give money. It's not because they feel guilty or pressured, but because this is how they support their family.

WEEK 4: A NEW RESPONSIBILITY

Why This Storyline Helps

Now, let's zoom out and take all of this in. God is our Father who, through the cross, has adopted us into his family who love and serve one another.

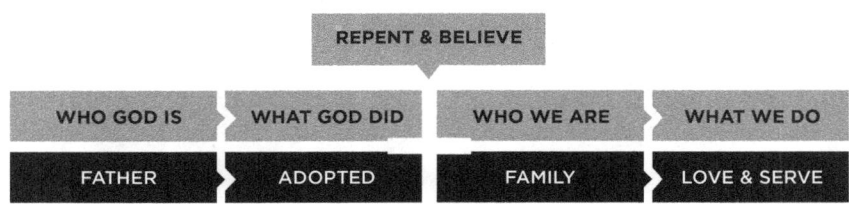

Knowing the whole storyline is essential.

When we start to think (and more importantly act) as if our relationships in church, our ministries, or small groups, are the same as any other low-commitment group, we may struggle with what it looks like to live as a family, and that can manifest itself in a variety of different ways. Some of us might have a tendency to speak poorly of another believer when they've disappointed us. Maybe we've noticed a private struggle that one of our group members is experiencing but don't know how to help and leave it at that. Or, maybe some of us get scared and defensive when we think about doing more than filling a seat on Sunday.

How do we combat this way of thinking? One way people try is by simply to focusing on the behavior. For example, consider the issue of speaking ill of someone. We can open the Bible to Ephesians 4:29, "Let no corrupting talk come out of your mouths." It's true Ephesians 4:29 says that, and the Bible has many other warnings against speaking ill about others. But that might not be a very helpful way to confront someone with the hope that they would repent. "The Bible says so!" just focuses on activity, without consideration for the heart behind the behavior.

AN INTRODUCTION TO **GOSPEL-CENTERED DISCIPLESHIP**

If we select verses like Ephesians 4:29 that talk about gossip and remove them from their context, we risk focusing on the activity alone. At times, this is appropriate. A follower of Jesus should care enough about the Bible's commands that we find them compelling. But we know that often we need more than just a rule to follow. And thankfully, God gives us so much more than rules throughout the entire Bible — even in Ephesians 4.

As we introduced in the previous lesson, our strategy is to work backwards through the storyline. Using that strategy with this gospel storyline, let's go back to Ephesians 4. But this time let's start in verse 22, where Paul first describes what happens to you through the gospel. He says in Christ you were taught...

> *to put off your old self, which belongs to your former manner of life and is corrupt through deceitful desires, and to be renewed in the spirit of your minds, and to put on the new self, created after the likeness of God in true righteousness and holiness. Therefore, having put away falsehood, let each one of you speak the truth with his neighbor, for we are members one of another.*
>
> Ephesians 4:22-25

The cross makes us a family. It's out of that gospel identity that Paul says in verse 29, "Let no corrupting talk come out of your mouths, but only such as is good for building up, as fits the occasion, that it may give grace to those who hear."

Our words should give grace to those who hear them, because we've put on the new self, created after the likeness of God in true righteousness and holiness, and are members one of another. We're family, because we've been adopted by our Father through Christ. We have a new responsibility to each other that isn't based merely on what we do, but on who we are.

It can change everything when you're given a reason to speak in loving and uplifting ways that are rooted in something more profound than guilt, pressure, or just "because the Bible says so." When we can connect a command to its roots in the gospel, it gets to the inward heart of the matter, instead of just addressing the outward behaviors.

What Devotion Looks Like

The gospel storyline of how we relate to the church is all about a new responsibility we have because of our new identity in Christ.

God showed his devotion to us by sending his son to take our sin on the cross, providing a way for us to be forgiven and reconciled to God. That's why we seek to identify our spiritual gifts and use them to serve, why we're committed to biblical community, even when it's tough, why we support the church financially, and why we're committed to resolve conflicts in God-honoring ways.

All of these activities are motivated by understanding that our identity and activity are rooted in the gospel.

There's a man who has been a part of our church with his family almost since its establishment. While he would say it's been a good run for him and his family, it hasn't been without struggles. For example, decisions were made by our church leaders they wouldn't have chosen, and sometimes it led to real hurt. But he and his family stayed faithfully committed to this church and its mission. When asked what had caused them to stay when it would have been easy to leave, he simply stated, "Because that's what family does." That's godliness. That's maturity. That's spiritual growth.

May we always remember this gospel truth that through the cross, we have a father who adopted us as family who love and serve.

04

WEEKLY EXERCISE

Think about someone in the church that you could serve or encourage this week. It can be someone in your group, someone you serve with, or someone you see serving.

Write them an encouraging note, give them a gift, offer to pray for them, or do something that would serve them.

05

A NEW PURPOSE

Read 2 Corinthians 5:17-21

What does this passage say about our identity in Christ?
_____
_____
_____

What did God do for us according to this passage?
_____
_____
_____

What does "the message of reconciliation" mean?
_____
_____
_____

What do ambassadors do?
_____
_____
_____

How are we ambassadors for Christ?
_____
_____
_____

What is the outcome for others when we share the message we are given to share?
_____
_____
_____

All this is from God, who through Christ reconciled us to himself and gave us the ministry of reconciliation; that is, in Christ God was reconciling the world to himself, not counting their trespasses against them, and entrusting to us the message of reconciliation.

—2 Corinthians 5:18-19

WEEK 5: A NEW PURPOSE

05

Larry Walters's infamous story began with a lawn chair and a dream of flying. One day he purchased forty-five weather balloons from an Army-Navy surplus store. He filled the balloons with helium and strapped them, and himself, to the aluminum chair. With a pellet gun, some sandwiches and a six-pack of Miller Lite, Larry hoped the balloons would allow him to float thirty feet, or so, above his backyard, and enjoy a nice lunch. Then he would use the pellet gun to pop a few balloons so he could descend slowly back to earth.

But when Larry's friends cut his chair loose from its anchor, he launched into the Los Angeles sky as if he'd been shot from a cannon. He climbed and climbed and climbed until he finally leveled off at 16,000 feet! With his plan ruined, he found himself too afraid to shoot the balloons to lower his flying chair for fear that it might unbalance the load and get him into real trouble. He drifted for several hours, cold and alone, and eventually crossed into the approach corridor of LAX. Two airline pilots spotted him and radioed in the report of the flying man in a lawn chair.

Eventually, Walters gathered the nerve to shoot a few balloons. But his troubles were far from over. The cords hanging from his lawn chair tangled in some powerlines and caused a neighborhood to black out for twenty minutes. When he did finally step onto solid ground again, Larry was greeted by police officers and promptly arrested. As he was escorted away, a reporter asked why he did it. Larry looked at him and said, "A man can't just sit around."[1]

Purpose In Our Stories

People will do just about anything to bring some sense of purpose and meaning to their lives. When we begin to seek out a purpose for our lives, it is always found within a story. But what type of story? The stories that inspire meaning in our lives can be described in one of three ways.

Small Stories

In a small story, we are the center of all things — and we probably have a nice car and a white picket fence. Whether the small story is about pleasure, comfort, or control, it's ultimately about us. We like that, but it's not enough for us.

Grand Stories

Steve Jobs said to John Sculley when he was seeking to woo him away from Pepsi to work at Apple, "Do you want to sell sugar water for the rest of your life or do you want to come with me and change the world?" What an inspiration! Each of us can be part of grand stories that change the world. Grand stories reach beyond ourselves and may even reach beyond our lifetime, leaving a legacy of impact. It's a compelling thing to consider. But it's still not big enough for us.

God Stories

A God story includes eternal implications. Envision an eternal

---

[1] Northcutt, Wendy. "1982 At-Risk Survivor: Lawn Chair Larry." 1982 At-Risk Survivor: Lawn Chair Larry. Accessed October 03, 2016. http://www.darwinawards.com/stupid/stupid1998-11.html.

timeline with me. Imagine a line on the floor with a small dot on the end beside you. The line crosses the room and ends, as far as you can tell, at the door. But we know the line actually goes farther than that. Imagine we keep drawing the line out the door, across town, 800 miles to El Paso and then we keep drawing the line through the desert to California. We continue to Hawaii and then into space, past all the planets (even past Pluto, which doesn't even get to be a planet anymore). Our lives — even our grandest stories — all take place in that tiny dot beside you. God stories are the only stories that allow you to have a purpose that goes beyond that tiny little dot and touch eternity. God made you for eternity.

God's plan all long was that we would find our most profound sense of purpose in the eternally significant. Ecclesiastes 3:11 says, "he has put eternity into man's heart." Anything we devote our lives to that does not impact eternity will ultimately feel empty.

When we take part in God's story of redemption, we actually serve a purpose that goes beyond our own life, beyond our comfort, beyond our white picket fence existence, beyond our global neighborhood, and even beyond time as we know it: we participate in shaping eternity. But the only way we can ever commit to do what we are meant to do is by being compelled by the storyline of our gospel identity.

A Third Gospel Storyline

There is a story behind what we do. God has clearly revealed his identity as king and father throughout Scripture and in the person of his son. But there is a third way that disciples must know and experience God.

AN INTRODUCTION TO **GOSPEL-CENTERED DISCIPLESHIP**

God is Savior

But when the goodness and loving kindness of God our Savior appeared, he saved us, not because of works done by us in righteousness, but according to his own mercy, by the washing of regeneration and renewal of the Holy Spirit, whom he poured out on us richly through Jesus Christ our Savior.

Titus 3:4-6

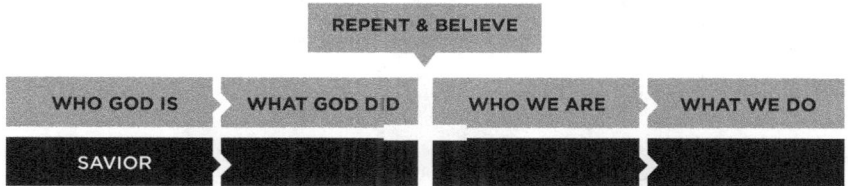

Hundreds of times in the Bible, God is called "Savior" or speaks of saving his people.

But what do we need to be saved from?

A favorite Christmas card says:

> If our greatest need had been information, God would have sent an educator.
> If our greatest need had been technology, God would have sent a scientist.
> If our greatest need had been money, God would have sent an economist.
> If our greatest need had been pleasure, God would have sent an entertainer.
> But our greatest need was forgiveness, so God sent a Savior.

WEEK 5: A NEW PURPOSE

We need to be saved from sin. In Matthew 1:21, Joseph hears an angel proclaim, "She will bear a son, and you shall call his name Jesus, for he will save his people from their sins."

God Sent Jesus

The cross was God's plan to sacrifice his son to rescue us from the penalty of sin, redeem us because sin enslaved us, reconcile us because sin separated us, justify us because sin condemned us, and restore us because sin shattered our lives.

The Father sent Jesus into the world on a rescue mission. This is the heart of the gospel and an essential truth all our beliefs are founded upon, but it isn't the end of the story. When Jesus appeared to his disciples following his resurrection, he didn't just enjoy their company, he gave them a mission.

> Jesus said to them again, "Peace be with you. As the Father has sent me, even so I am sending you." (John 20:21)

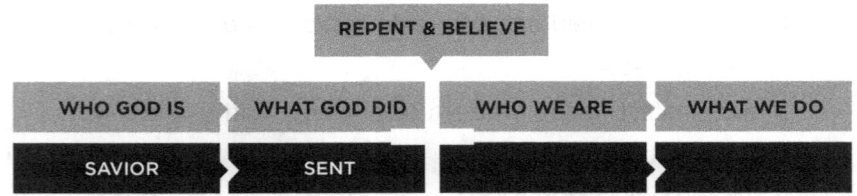

We Are Missionaries

As followers of Jesus, we are sent into our world to show people that God has come to redeem and restore all people and, ultimately, all things. We call sent people missionaries.

So, this is your new identity as a follower of Jesus Christ: You are a missionary.

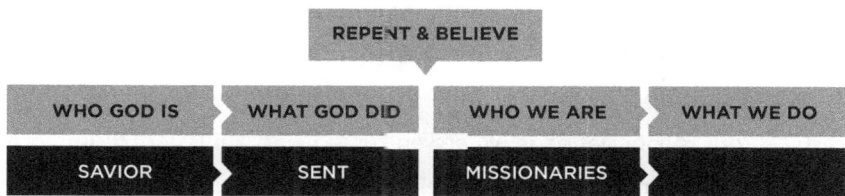

You might think, "I'm not a missionary. Missionaries are people who take their families to remote areas of Africa (or other places without Starbucks or frozen yogurt) to evangelize natives seen in National Geographic. Then you never hear from them again. That's a missionary. But that's not me!"

However, if you look up missionary in the dictionary, it just means "one sent on a mission." We are sent on a mission to our family, our neighborhood, our workplace, our schools, and every sphere of life. Simply, we are sent to wherever we are.

Some may question whether this truly applies to every follower of Jesus or just those sent to remote corners of the world. But Scripture addresses this issue without reservation.

> Therefore, if anyone is in Christ, he is a new creation. The old has passed away; behold, the new has come. All this is from God, who through Christ reconciled us to himself and gave us the ministry of reconciliation; that is, in Christ God was reconciling the world to himself, not counting their trespasses against them, and entrusting to us the message of reconciliation. Therefore, we are ambassadors for Christ, God making

his appeal through us. We implore you on behalf of Christ, be reconciled to God.

2 Corinthians 5:17-21

Everyone God saves, God sends. Just as Jesus explained in John 20:21, that the disciples would be sent in the same way he was, here we see Paul explain a similar parallel stating that *anyone* who is in Christ was reconciled to God through Christ's work. But that's not the whole story. The result of our reconciliation is we are entrusted with a mission: to implore others to be reconciled to God as well.

A New Identity Brings a New Purpose

As we prepared to start our second campus, the leaders of our children's ministry were meeting to plan the new campus set-up, which was going to be built around a space station theme.

In light of that, the children's ministry director introduced a woman to speak who was an accomplished astronaut and church member. In trying to give context to the space theme, the astronaut noted her numerous flights, NASA duties, and current responsibilities. Then she said, "But greater than that, I'm a member of the church." And she proceeded to talk about the mission of leading people to become fully devoted followers of Jesus Christ.

This famous person who was so admired for all she contributed to space exploration, said while that Grand Story is wonderful, it pales in comparison to making disciples. To her, helping others know Jesus was more important than anything she had done in her spectacular career. It wasn't that what this woman had accomplished in a rocket ship was unimportant, but only that it was less important than her part in God's story, which is the only story big enough for a person with eternity planted in her heart. Being a missionary gives us a new purpose; the greatest purpose of all.

Go and Multiply

Before Jesus ascended to heaven, he provided some clarity to his followers regarding their new purpose and what it would look like.

> Go therefore and make disciples of all nations, baptizing them in the name of the Father and of the Son and of the Holy Spirit, teaching them to observe all that I have commanded you. And behold, I am with you always, to the end of the age.
>
> Matthew 28:19-20

> But you will receive power when the Holy Spirit has come upon you, and you will be my witnesses in Jerusalem and in all Judea and Samaria, and to the end of the earth.
>
> Acts 1:8

So, if our new purpose is the ministry of reconciliation, how are we, as missionaries, to do this ministry? Jesus said the mission of the church is to participate in God's rescue mission by going into the world declaring the gospel in word and demonstrating its power in deed in the hopes that followers of Jesus will be multiplied as a result.

WEEK 5: A NEW PURPOSE

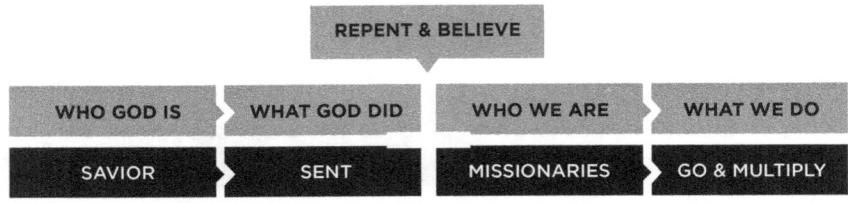

Practically, our church employs a variety of strategies to carry out this mission.

- **Top 5:** We pray for five people (though this number is merely a suggestion) in our lives who are not followers of Jesus. And we look for the opportunity to tell them about how Jesus Christ has made a difference in our lives through his death and resurrection, giving us a new identity as citizens and family.

- **Small Groups:** This is our church's strategy for making disciples. Small group leaders (or navigators) take on the responsibility of helping a dozen or so other people learn to follow Jesus Christ as his disciples.

- **Go-Ops (Go Opportunities):** Small groups actively serve people in our community by engaging with our local ministry partners. Our partners in ministry include: Galveston Urban Ministries, Galveston Street Ministry, Anchor Point Crisis Pregnancy Center, Friends through the Fight, Lighthouse Christian Ministries (for the most up-to-date list, visit our website at clearcreek.org)

- **Campus Launch Teams:** One of our campus pastors told me about a man who helped start the Clear Lake Campus. When he asked him to join the launch team, he said, "I knew my life had to be about something more than just my family, my job, and watching TV at night. I think this is it." He and others formed a core team that started a new campus in close proximity to their friends. Now we organize such teams for every new campus.

- **Church Planting:** We participate locally, nationally, and internationally in the planting of new churches. This includes trips to foreign countries by teams built to help church planters and their new congregations. It also includes helping people experience being on foreign soil in the name of Jesus for the first time.

In Matthew 4:19, Jesus said to his disciples, "Follow me and I will make you fishers of men." We must remember that to follow Jesus is to embrace the identity of a missionary whose activity is to go all over the world (including our local community) and multiply disciples. When we do this, we take part in God's story!

Things to Consider

Being sent into the world with the message and ministry of reconciliation makes a lot of people feel uncomfortable; and for good reason. After all, when we talk about people needing to be saved it sounds like something is wrong with them. It sounds like they are in a perilous condition. And we all know how well messages like those are normally received. But the fact is that people are in trouble and their souls are in a perilous condition.

So, we must not get shortsighted and redefine the Christian message with something that's a little more comfortable for us. We must not allow the mission of the local church to be diminished.

The church is not a self-improvement seminar. When we see the church this way, we just want to use it to make our lives a little better; we want to be told how to have good kids, less stress, more comfort and happiness, pretty weddings and touching funerals. Just a little something to add meaning to everyone's white-picket-fence world. In this sense, the church is part of a small story.

The church is not a social service institution. When we believe that the church's responsibility is to make the world a better place, we commit to good works like feeding the poor, practicing social justice, and being part of humanitarian aid efforts. These things are good and important, but if that's all we do, then we fall short of God's plan for our lives and force the church into a deceptively short-term-focused role in a grand story.

The church is a rescue squad sent on a mission from God. This is a mission that will touch people's lives personally and influence our culture globally, but it will also impact eternity. It is the only story that will matter five minutes after you die and still matter a million years later. Everyone lives forever somewhere, and our ministry can impact another's eternity.

The Christian faith is a viral movement. You heard about Jesus' death on the cross for your sins and his resurrection power from someone. And they heard it from someone too. When the gospel came to you, it was on its way to someone else.

It must not stop with us.

When we don't live as a missionary, we are short-circuiting God's plan for our lives, and choosing a story that will not satisfy our hearts. But we get easily intoxicated with our small story or grand story. It's visible. It's immediate. The apostle Paul warns against this on numerous occasions.

> *As for you, always be sober-minded, endure suffering, do the work of an evangelist, fulfill your ministry.*
>
> 2 Timothy 4:5

If you don't have a strong desire to participate in God's mission, remem-

AN INTRODUCTION TO **GOSPEL-CENTERED DISCIPLESHIP**

ber, work backwards through the story. Belief changes behavior. Identity informs activity. You are a missionary. But if you don't see yourself as a missionary, revisit the fact that God sent you. And if you don't see yourself as sent by God, go back to the gospel truth of God being a savior who chose to save you. When we see God as a savior who, in Christ, rescued us from sin, we better understand that everyone God saves, God sends. And if we are sent, that makes us a missionary. And if we are missionaries, that means we are charged with a mission to go and multiply.

05

WEEKLY EXERCISE

Think about and pray for your Top 5.

Write the names of five people you hope will come to faith in Jesus.

1. _____
2. _____
3. _____
4. _____
5. _____

Take a few minutes right now to pray for each person on your list.

Ask God to give you an opportunity to serve them, invite them to a church service, or share the gospel with them this week.

Intentionally seek out an opportunity to serve, invite, or share the gospel with one of these five people.

06

GROWTH, GROUP, AND GOSPEL FLUENCY

Read Galatians 5:16-25

What does Paul call the Galatians to do in the opening verse?
_____
_____
_____

What does it mean to "walk by the Spirit?"
_____
_____
_____

What does the passage say are the benefits of walking in the Spirit?
_____
_____
_____

To whom, in verse 24, is this life available?
_____
_____
_____

What does this say about change?
_____
_____
_____

What does verse 25 say about our role concerning real change?
_____
_____
_____

And those who belong to Christ Jesus have crucified the flesh with its passions and desires. If we live by the Spirit, let us also keep in step with the Spirit.

—Galatians 5:24-25

WEEK 6: GROWTH, GROUP, AND GOSPEL FLUENCY

06

When my son Beckett was nine years old, I (Yancey) caught him rubbing his stomach and looking disappointed. I asked him what he was doing and he said, "Dad, I think I need to get in shape." He then proceeded to run on our treadmill – for less than five minutes! When I asked him if he felt like he was in shape now, he confidently responded, "Yep, I'm done."

My son believed he had changed, but he really hadn't. It's not that he couldn't change. He simply didn't know how change happens. He's not alone.

Many people assume that if they just attend a church service, pray a little more, or start some other spiritual activity, deep change will come. They believe they'll have a greater sense of purpose, feel abiding peace, and walk in spiritual power. Unfortunately, many fail to experience any authentic, long-lasting improvement.

A Gospel Approach to Change

Can real change happen? Yes! Let's look at a passage in the Bible which deals with change. The apostle Paul tells the Galatians:

> *But I say, walk by the Spirit, and you will not gratify the desires*

> of the flesh. For the desires of the flesh are against the Spirit, and the desires of the Spirit are against the flesh, for these are opposed to each other, to keep you from doing the things you want to do. But if you are led by the Spirit, you are not under the law. Now the works of the flesh are evident: sexual immorality, impurity, sensuality, idolatry, sorcery, enmity, strife, jealousy, fits of anger, rivalries, dissensions, divisions, envy, drunkenness, orgies, and things like these. I warn you, as I warned you before, that those who do such things will not inherit the kingdom of God. But the fruit of the Spirit is love, joy, peace, patience, kindness, goodness, faithfulness, gentleness, self-control; against such things there is no law. And those who belong to Christ Jesus have crucified the flesh with its passions and desires.
>
> Galatians 5:16-24

Do you see what Paul claims about spiritual transformation? Life in God, which Paul calls walking by the Spirit, is a life where you increasingly move from "works of the flesh" such as impurity, envy, and other sins to a life full of the "fruit of the Spirit" such as love, joy, and peace. The Bible's message is clear: You can change! You can grow in your devotion to God in a way that makes a life-changing difference.

That's why Paul concludes in verse 25, "If we live by the Spirit, let us also keep in step with the Spirit." In other words, if by grace God in Christ has done his work in you, then continue to live a life which fosters that work.

This study has presented a way to think about growing our devotion to God with an approach rooted in the storyline of the gospel: who God is and what God did for us in Jesus has made us who we are and changed what we do as followers of Jesus. But those truths won't be as meaningful to us until we truly understand how growth happens and how people change.

WEEK 6: GROWTH, GROUP, AND GOSPEL FLUENCY

Truths to Believe

Behind every sin is a lie that we've chosen to believe over what God has already established. Earlier we discussed how this strategy was used by Satan from the very beginning.

In Genesis 3, Eve believed the serpent's lie in the garden and ate the forbidden fruit. Satan even stated it this way, "Did God actually say, 'You shall not eat of any tree in the garden?'" Satan knew that if he could get Eve to doubt the veracity of God's word, then he could get her to sin. She knew she had everything she needed and that God had promised judgment if they disobeyed, but she chose to trust her own desires and the serpent's claims instead. Ultimately, in that moment of sin, she was believing the lie that God was not acting in her best interest. We've been suffering for it ever since. However, we can't pin it all on Eve. Every sin that has ever been committed is rooted in believing the lies which prop up those sins.

Most of us ignore the impact of belief when we pursue spiritual change. We commonly think spiritual growth is simply about putting some elbow grease into a few behaviors and then expecting results. The problem with a behavior-oriented approach to spiritual change is that it forgets to deal with the underlying reasons for those sins.

It is possible for people with a long "To-Do" list to change if they're enthusiastic about accomplishing those goals. But what often happens when these emotionally-driven motivations settle back to normal levels is just like the typical New Year's resolution and the change doesn't stick. If we depend on our ability to remain emotionally charged to see long-term change without addressing underlying causes for our struggles, it's ultimately a plan for frustration, depression, and bitterness.

AN INTRODUCTION TO GOSPEL-CENTERED DISCIPLESHIP

That's why we must move past merely dealing with behaviors, and into the beliefs supporting them. In other words, what are our hearts really trusting when we sin?

Trust Before Try

Let's be clear: gospel change is not opposed to trying, it's just not where we start. We begin with our beliefs, what our hearts are trusting in, and then we see the impact that this trust has on the things in which we try. Simply put, we are more likely to experience long-term change when we focus on beliefs before behaviors.

If believers are to walk in obedience and experience change, they must replace the lies their hearts believe with God's truth. As our hearts feed on God's Word rather than the falsehoods of Satan, we begin to delight in God and his Word, and grow in our desire to obey the Lord.

To read the New Testament is to see that the highest truths flow from what God has done for us in the good news of Jesus. The gospel is chiefly where we see God's magnificent grace for his people. That's why it's also the focus of the Spiritual Growth Grid — a tool centered upon the person and work of Jesus that not only shows what we do in order to grow as a disciple of Jesus, but why we do those things. *Why should I listen and obey? Why should I love and serve? Why should I go and multiply?*

Spiritual growth always starts with the gospel.

Gospel-First Groups

To be a "gospel-first" community is to be a group of believers who consistently directs others to the gospel of grace, proclaiming that all of the things we seek (identity, worth, security) are already ours, not because of what we've earned but because of what Jesus' death earned for us. This is a critical key to real change and our desire for every CCCC group.

Leveraging small group as a place to faithfully remind each other of, and strengthen each other in, the work of Jesus for us is one way we can press the gospel into ourselves and our fellow believers. This results in the deepest kind of change because both our head and heart are impacted. Thus, gospel-centered groups begin not by addressing our trying for Jesus but with our trusting in Jesus. If we want to grow well with other fully devoted followers of Jesus, we must learn to go to the gospel first.

This demands that gospel-centered groups become fluent in the gospel.

Growing Your Gospel Fluency[1]

Fluency simply means expressing oneself accurately, easily, and effectively. To be fluent in the gospel is to have the ability to bring the person and work of Jesus Christ to the issues you and the people in your group face. Pastor and author Jeff Vandersteldt puts it this way:

> In order to effectively equip your missional community in Gospel Fluency, you will need to create a culture where it is

---

[1] This section influenced by Vandersteldt, Jeff. "Gospel Fluency." GCM Collective. Accessed October 03, 2016. http://www.gcmcollective.org/article/gospel-fluency/.

normal to speak the gospel to each other regularly. Every sin and issue that stands in the way of our faithfulness to Jesus' commands is ultimately a gospel issue, since sin is the outcome of unbelief in Jesus (John 16:9). One of your key jobs will be to equip your people to know the Gospel, apply it to all of life, and speak it to each other.

Know. Apply. Speak. These three practices are foundational to gospel fluency. This will necessitate the group regularly checking members' motives, beliefs, and actions to see if they reflect faith in Jesus or in someone or something else (i.e., our idols).

When we find areas in our heart and life where we struggle to believe the work of Jesus for us we need other believers to remind us how the gospel provides for our sufficiency in Christ, lead us to repent of any false beliefs and practices, and call us to more deeply believe in Jesus' work toward that specific issue. This is what it means to apply the gospel.

The more frequently we know, apply, and speak the gospel to each other in group, the more habitual a practice it will become in both group times and everyday life.

Here are three ways to grow your gospel fluency:

> **Think "gospel first!"** If the temptation is to work on behavior before belief, then when someone is dealing with behavioral issues we should fight the temptation by asking, "How does the gospel address this?" and "What about the gospel are you not believing?" Effective small groups continually think "gospel first."
>
> **Rehearse the gospel and restate the Grid.** The storylines in

the Spiritual Growth Grid highlight our gospel identities and clarify how they support and instruct the behaviors of a disciple. These storylines can be easily forgotten by hearts seeking to justify themselves by achievement instead of the finished work of Christ.

Connect beliefs to behaviors. Learn to help group members identify any idols (people, ideas, or things looked to for security, worth, or identity) by linking their "trust issues" to their "try issues". Connect their behavior to their beliefs, then compare and contrast those beliefs to those rooted in the gospel of Jesus. Work backward through the Grid to expose beliefs.

Working Backwards Through the Grid

The key to deep change is finding the conflicts in your heart: our behavior struggles will always point to our belief struggles.

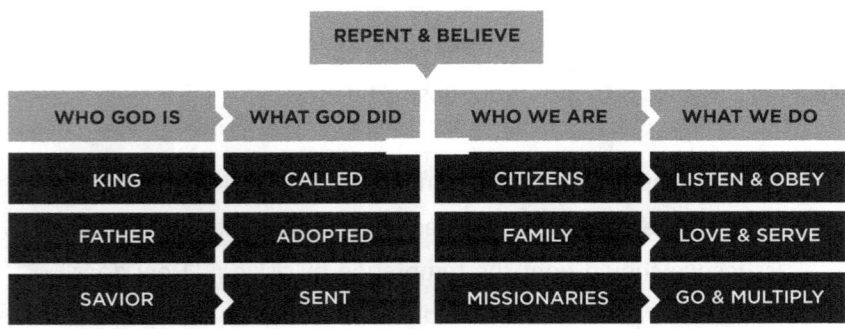

Working backwards through the three gospel storylines of the Spiritual Growth Grid begins with behavior ("What We Do" column) then moves to the beliefs ("Who God Is", "What God Did", "Who We Are" columns)

connected with them, seeking to discover any places of struggle in our hearts to believe.

Using the grid in this way is an attempt to identify any areas where we need to repent of false beliefs and more deeply believe the treasures of the gospel for ourselves. As we noted earlier in this study, this is why repenting and believing isn't just the first step in a life of devotion to Jesus but integral to every step afterward.

Here are possible examples of push backs to the storylines presented in the Grid:

Who God Is: I struggle with God as Father; my father was horrible.
What God Did: God sent us? Well, that's probably true for pastors only.
Who I Am: I don't see myself as a member of God's family; I just go to church.

The importance of the Spiritual Growth Grid is that it shows us truths to be believed rather than mere behaviors to do. The aim of the disciple is to believe by faith that these gospel statements are true. We are depending upon the Holy Spirit to apply these truths to our hearts and empower us to listen and obey, love and serve, and go and multiply.

Here is a step-by-step way to work backwards using the Grid:

1. Identify which "What We Do" area (Listen & Obey, Love & Serve, Go & Multiply) you struggle with and examine the corresponding Gospel Storyline (Who We Are, What God Did, Who God Is).

2. Ask how deeply you believe each of the truths of Who We Are, What God Did, and Who God Is. We are attempting to discover how strongly our hearts are connected to gospel realities.

WEEK 6: GROWTH, GROUP, AND GOSPEL FLUENCY

Let's practice: On the chart below, circle each area on the storyline where you find a struggle to believe, then rate the depth of belief you have in the circled areas on a scale from 1 to 4 (four being greatest) and write that number on the Spiritual Growth Grid.

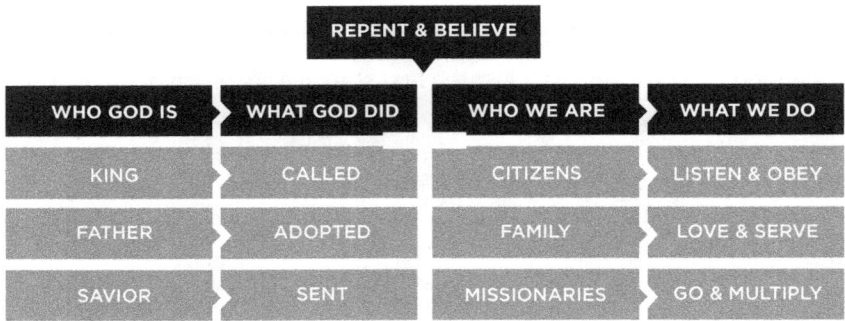

3. Ask diagnostic questions that probe the depth of the conflict with believing the truths of the gospel storyline. For example:

   - What do you think of when you hear the word "father?"
   - What was your father like?
   - Did you have any siblings growing up? How did you interact with them?
   - What kind of family dynamic did you have during childhood?
   - How do you see the gathered church?
   - What do you think of other Christians?

4. If Navigators feel someone needs further teaching concerning a specific area, they can suggest an extracurricular growth plan that deepens the member in their belief in the gospel storyline they're struggling with. Navigators might consider studying biblical passages or books with the group member or finding a helpful activity to accomplish.

   For example, in trying to increase the depth of belief in our identity as members of God's family, the Navigator might challenge the group member with one or more of these assignments:

- Passage: Study 1 Cor. 12-14 and reflect with Navigator.
- Book: Read Steve Timmis's *Total Church* and discuss with Navigator.
- Activity: Serve somewhere temporarily and reflect with Navigator.

5. Periodically review the Grid (and any additional growth plans) with the goal to encourage, facilitate, and support in moving one step deeper in belief regarding the areas of struggle.

Remember, go to the gospel first! Let the behavior issues expose the belief issues. We are seeking to get at the root of the conflict with the power of the gospel; not merely dealing with the effects but the cause behind them.

Behavior modification is not the goal. Our aim is to more deeply trust in the person and work of Jesus in order that the Holy Spirit would empower our lives for God's glory. The more, by faith, we repent and believe in the truths of the gospel, the more our lives change by the grace of God and the power of the Spirit. This is the kind of growth we want to see in small groups.

WEEK 6: GROWTH, GROUP, AND GOSPEL FLUENCY

An Overview of Devoted

This book serves as in introduction to a new small group study series we're calling *Devoted: Discipleship Training for Small Groups*. Groups will spend two years working through studies that focus on the three gospel storylines of the Spiritual Growth Grid and their impact upon the life of a disciple.

As you might imagine, groups who choose to work through the Devoted study series are committing themselves to the time and effort required to grow in the Spiritual Growth Grid. With each study, participants will be expected to work through:

- Scripture memory of 2-4 verses
- Three days of teaching per week culminating with a weekly exercise
- Additional study if necessary as recommended by the Navigator
- All of this with a 'gospel-first' perspective

Navigators will lead weekly meetings where the group will share what they've learned and practiced. Each week, groups will work through discussions concerning weekly studies which focus on Repent and Believe, Listen and Obey, Love and Serve, and Go and Multiply in order to become better trained into the life of a follower of Jesus.

The studies will train you in the eight critical practices of a disciple-making disciple.

Year 1: Relying on God's power, hearing God's voice, living interdependently, and sharing the gospel in word and deed.

Year 2: Loving God with all your heart, submitting to God's will, serving

AN INTRODUCTION TO **GOSPEL-CENTERED DISCIPLESHIP**

more than being served, and sharing the gospel.

Join Us as We Follow Jesus Together

We hope all of this makes your heart beat faster! This is an opportunity not only to grow in Christ but to do so in a way that equips you to help others do the same in the future. It is our prayer and goal that in committing to this spiritual formation process you will become a disciple-making disciple, replicable in a reproducible method, grounded in the gospel of Jesus. We recognize some may decline this invitation for various reasons. Maybe some are not ready for the depth of commitment, cannot give the time required, or believe they need to start with a different group. We understand that completely. But if you want to master the eight critical practices of a follower of Jesus, deepen yourself in your gospel identity and its implications for your life, and be trained not only to be a disciple of Jesus but learn how to train others to do the same, this study is for you!

Ready to get started? If so, it's time to take your next step to become a disciple-making disciple.

06

WEEKLY EXERCISE

In lesson 6, we concluded the Introduction to Gospel-Centered Discipleship by noting that we really can change. We can grow in our devotion to Jesus. However, we must focus on belief before behavior. Our call is to first deeply trust what God has done for us and said about our identity before we can truly grow. One of the ways to practice this is by walking backwards through the three gospel storylines looking for areas where we need to repent and believe more deeply.

Reflect on the Spiritual Growth Grid and this introduction to gospel-centered discipleship. Which of the behavior areas is the deepest source of struggle for you?

_____
_____
_____

Working backwards through that gospel storyline, in which related area of belief do you most need to deepen your faith?

_____
_____
_____

Write the Scripture passage for that square on a card and memorize it this week. Ask God to help you replace lies you find yourself believing with the truth of Scripture.

_____
_____
_____

REPENT & BELIEVE

WHO GOD IS	WHAT GOD DID	WHO WE ARE	WHAT WE DO
KING Psalm 47:7-8	CALLED 1 Corinthians 1:26-27	CITIZENS Colossians 1:13-14	LISTEN & OBEY Psalm 1:1-3
FATHER 1 Corinthians 8:6	ADOPTED John 1:12	FAMILY Leviticus 26:11-12	LOVE & SERVE Galatians 5:13
SAVIOR Luke 2:10-11	SENT Romans 10:14-15	MISSIONARIES 2 Timothy 4:1-2	GO & MULTIPLY Matthew 28:19-20

www.ingramcontent.com/pod-product-compliance
Lightning Source LLC
Chambersburg PA
CBHW061336040426
42444CB00011B/2941